Go For It!

MAKE YOUR LIFE
COUNT FOR GOD

 Elk Lake
Publishing, Inc.

Plymouth, Massachusetts

Endorsements

"*Go For It!* reminds readers that God has a plan and purpose for their lives. With interactive questions, and space to write, readers will embark on a journey toward self-reflection. When they are finished, they will have answered the questions every person desperately wants to know: Who am I? Who is God? and How Does He want to use me?"

—**Michelle Lazurek**, author "*An Invitation to the Table*"

"I read all the way through Poppy's book and it is REALLY a wonderful blueprint for women to find their DREAM purpose."

—**Heidi McLaughlin** International Speaker and Author, Heart Connection Ministry | Member of Radiant Team

"Do you ever feel stuck in life? Desiring purpose and fulfillment, but not exactly sure how to get there? Look no further than Poppy Smith's new book "*Go For It!—Make Your Life Count for God*" This is a treasure trove of wise encouragement coupled with very practical steps you can begin today. Working through the lists and applications here is like partnering with your very own Life Coach. Poppy brings all her experiences, knowledge, faith commitment and stories together so that we are able to better discern the unique life God has for each of us. Don't just sit around, get a copy now and *Go For It!*"

—**Lucinda Secrest McDowell**, author of **"*Dwelling Places*"** EncouragingWords.net

"Women today are seeking spiritual answers with heightened enthusiasm. *Go For It!*, by Poppy Smith meets those needs on a personal level and dares the reader to DREAM bigger than she has before. Spiritual truth outlines Poppy's *dare*, equipping each woman with a foundation she can trust as her dreams become a reality."

Linda Goldfarb, Owner of Live Powerfully Now LLC,
Co/Founder of Parenting Awesome Kids,
Author of *Loving the ME God Sees,* International Speaker,
Certified *Relationship Mentor/Coach to Parents and Women*
www.LivePowerfullyNow.org

"As soon as I started reading *Go For It!*, I was inspired! If you're looking to discover your passion and purpose so that you can live life more abundantly – this is your book! In her unique and delightful style, Poppy invites you to live a God-directed, God-empowered, and God-fulfilled life that impacts others!"

—**Becky Harling,** International Speaker,
John Maxwell Certified Coach and
the author of *How to Listen, So People will Talk*

"*Go For It!* is for anyone who wonders if her life has real worth. Poppy Smith has fashioned a hope-filled guide to find answers to life's most compelling questions: What am I living for? Do I have worth? How can I know God's purposes for me? Why am I here? How can I move beyond past failures? Do I dare to dream big dreams? Through inspiring stories and examples, Poppy Smith challenges readers to stretch themselves to be who God has designed them to be. The pages of this book encourage, give guidance, touch hearts, and convince those who do choose to *Go For It!* that the path of self-discovery is worth taking."

—**Maxine Marsolini,** *Author and Life Coach,*
Rebuilding Families, *Building Today,*
Strengthening Tomorrow, www.rebuildingfamilies.net

Go For It! Make Your Life Count For God
Poppy Smith | **Elk Lake Publishing**

Copyright © 2016 by Poppy Smith

Requests for information should be addressed to:
Elk Lake Publishing, Inc., Plymouth, MA 02360

ISBN-13 Number: 978-1-944430-64-1

Cover: Jeff Gifford
Interior Design: Melinda Martin
Editors: Susan K. Stewart, Deb Haggerty

Contents

Introduction

Live a life worthy of the calling you have received

Ephesians 4:1

- Do you wonder what God created you to do?

- Do you want to explore and find direction?

- Do you have desires and dreams but wonder where to go with them?

If your heart is saying yes, then this book is for you.

- You'll be inspired to soar, to risk, to D.R.E.A.M.

- You'll discover how you're uniquely wired by God to live a fulfilling life.

- You'll uncover the role your strengths, talents, and life-shaping experiences play in God's plans and purposes for you.

- You'll find GO FOR IT! an easy-to-read, life-changing guide based on Biblical principles. With personal stories, Scriptures, insightful questions, and helpful exercises in every chapter, you'll learn to identify your own uniqueness.

- You'll also discover how God has shaped you into the woman you are today.

As you work through this book, by yourself, with a close friend, or with a small group, I encourage you to stop, chew over what you're reading, and answer the questions sprinkled throughout each chapter. In this way, you'll create your own life map that incorporates your past, your present, and where God wants to take you in the future. So let me encourage you to D.R.E.A.M.

- **Dare to Dream.** What might God have for you no matter your past experiences, your age, or your stage of life? Think without self-imposed limits. Let your heart sing and your mind soar as you cry out to God, "Show me your purposes for my life. What have you put in me that you want to nourish and develop?"

- **Review your life.** Look back and trace God's hand on your journey so far. Have events, experiences, people, or books impacted you? How? Discover your strengths, your successes, and what fulfills you. Identify how God has been shaping your life to make you who you are.

- **Explore opportunities.** Think outside the box. What makes you come alive? What new pathways and possibilities could you explore? What excites you? What fits your passions, interests, and strengths? Learn Biblical keys to making good choices.

- **Anticipate obstacles.** Both internal and external obstacles are inevitable. Saying yes to God requires perseverance and trust that He will provide solutions. Be prepared to have your faith stretched as you learn to overcome your own fearful self-talk and tackle practical obstacles.

- **Move forward.** Invite God to direct your steps and help you make a plan of action. Let him stretch your faith, deepen your trust, and surprise you with his amazing blessings.

Are you ready to plunge in? Ready to *GO FOR IT*? Then, let's get moving and see where God wants to take you.

Chapter One:
Dare to Dream

We are God's workmanship, created in Christ Jesus to do good works which God prepared in advance for us to do.

Ephesians 2:10

Your Life Is a God-Given Treasure—Value It!

If you inherited five million dollars, what would you do with it?

- Would you spend it? Maybe on a special vacation, jewelry, designer clothes, or luxury items?

- Would you share it? Giving to your family, your church, the poor, or charitable organizations?

- Would you invest it? Benefitting both yourself and others over the years ahead?

Millions of people would love to face this dilemma. But, have *you* ever realized your life is worth so much more than five million dollars?

Your life is a gift from God.

Moses, the man God appointed to lead the Israelites out of Egypt and into the Promised Land, was intensely aware of time passing. He cried out to God, *Teach us to number our days and recognize how few they are; help us to spend them as we should* (Psalm 90 :12).

Our human tendency is to think life will go on forever, but it won't. Time passes, and we can't capture it or slow it down. It can't be retrieved and reinvested. It's like a coin. You can only spend it once.

If you're in your twenties or thirties, you're fortunate. You could have many years ahead in which to wisely invest your life. On the other hand, maybe you've already used up a lot of your capital. Regardless of your age right now, you can't change how you've invested your life so far. But you can make intentional choices from now on. And that's what this book is about.

Unlike Eastern religions that claim karma allows you to be born again and again, the Bible makes clear you only live once (Hebrews 9:27). You won't get another opportunity to explore and experience all God has prepared for you.

Now is the time to live your best possible life. Now is the time to reflect on the following:

What have I done so far with the dreams, longings, strengths, and talents God has given me?

_____

_____

_____

_____

_____

Chapter One: Dare to Dream

How might God want you to spend the years ahead?

_____

_____

_____

_____

_____

Who Are You Living For?

Have you ever read a story that made you stop and think about your own life? Let me share one with you:

Jane lived a safe life. She didn't want to risk anything, whether that meant being hurt, dealing with needy people, or failing to achieve what she'd set her heart on. If she was going to stay safe from life's disappointments, she knew she had to be careful with her heart, her desires, and her commitments. Taking care of herself was her first priority.

So she made three life-shaping choices:

1. Jane decided not to love others because it was too costly.

To love meant giving up what she valued most, her carefully constructed, safe and uncomplicated life. It could bring problems and possibly unpleasant, messy relationships. After thinking about it, she decided she would be better off avoiding involvement with others and just do what she preferred.

The result? Jane became self-absorbed and missed the joy of deep friendships and love.

2. Jane then decided not to dream too much.

She refused to have hopes and longings because she believed they didn't get you anywhere and only brought disappointment. Better to do what came in a given day than long for something more.

The result? Jane never discovered her potential or the purpose God had created her for.

3. Jane also decided not to serve others.

She felt inadequate to help anyone. Besides, getting involved with people and their needs would be a nuisance and inconvenient. People could take care of themselves or turn to others who liked to help. It would just take too much time and effort.

The result? Jane missed the blessing that comes when you share your heart, your gifts, and what you have with others.

One day Jane died. Appearing before God, she proudly said, "Here is my life."

And God said, "What life?"[1]

Choices: Gift and Responsibility

As women in the twenty-first century, you and I face choices never before available.

For the most part, we can choose our direction in life. We can:

- Marry or not.

- Love a husband, leave a husband, or have many husbands in one lifetime.

---

1   Michael Tan, *Lose and Find,* (Vantagepoint Magazine, Jan.-Feb. 2005.).

Chapter One: Dare to Dream

- Pursue our own ambitions.

- Have children or not.

- Be an at-home mother, work outside the home, or both.

- Live where we want, get the education we want, pursue the career we want.

- Live for God's purposes or for our own.

- Choose the kind of person we want to be.

- Become a different person.

- Be set free from what holds us back.

- Live a life focused on loving God and others.

Jane's choices not only determined the course of her life, but they also shaped who she became.

Her choice not to love too much, dream too much, or step out of her safe place and serve others, turned her into a scared, self-protective woman. Jane chose to limit her world by saying *no* to what life offered.

Do you identify with her? Would you say you're inclined to be hesitant? Are you more likely to opt for the familiar and resist situations that might stretch you? If you do tend to choose what's safe and predictable, could you be missing out on some opportunities to grow and serve?

Perhaps you don't identify with Jane at all. Maybe you're more likely to be hasty. You love to jump into what seems exciting, often without considering whether you're remotely suited for this particular opportunity. Or if you even have time to add one more thing.

Which response is more typical of you? Are you hesitant or hasty? Jot down how you see yourself, and why.

I'm more inclined to hesitate because:

_____

_____

_____

_____

_____

I'm more inclined to be hasty because:

_____

_____

_____

_____

_____

I confess, I have a tendency to be hasty because I love the stimulation of doing something new. But I'm not always wise. Proverbs 14:8 says, *The wisdom of the prudent is to give thought to their ways.* How true.

Chapter One: Dare to Dream

I Think I'll Do Something Else

One year I agreed to teach a women's weekly Bible study at a local church, something I love to do. However, by Christmas, I was feeling restless and asked the women's director to see if someone else would like to take over. My goal was not to laze around but to take some classes at a nearby Bible college instead.

A newly returned missionary was asked and immediately agreed. Everything seemed to be working out just as I'd hoped. But, as I looked at the college catalog, I realized that the classes I wanted to take weren't available on the days I was free. A sinking feeling came over me as I realized I had run ahead of God and chosen my own path, once again.

A short time after realizing that I'd been too impulsive, the phone rang. The women's ministry director told me that my replacement was having emergency surgery with a long recovery ahead of her. I sensed what was coming. With a little hesitancy, she asked if I could possibly reconsider and come back for the rest of the year. What could I say?

I wish I could declare I've never acted impulsively again, but that wouldn't be true. Nor would it help you. Growth in becoming wiser and more dependent on God's direction takes time. But I am trying.

Whether you're inclined to hesitate or hastily rush into whatever new, exciting opportunity opens up, God made you for a purpose. *It's in Christ that we find out who we are and what we are to live for. Long before we first heard of Christ ... he had his eye on us, had designs on us for glorious living, part of the overall purpose he is working out in everything and everyone* (Ephesians 1:11, MSG).

Go For It!

God's Word Makes It Clear That He Created You.

- The psalmist, David, declared, *You created my inmost being; you knit me together in my mother's womb. I praise you because I am fearfully and wonderfully made* (Psalm 139: 13-14a).

- Through Isaiah, God declared, *I am your Creator. You were in my care even before you were born* (Isaiah 44:2, CEV).

You have worth in God's eyes. He made you to:

- Know him: To receive His forgiveness, have his power in your life, and to live eternally (1 John 1: 8-9; Ephesians 3:20; John 17:3).

- Love him: With all your heart, soul, mind, and strength (Mark 12:30).

- Serve him: Going into the world around you—whether near or far—and doing the good works He prepared for you (Philippians 2:10).

- Accept his view of you: He counts your life as having great value to him and to others. His love gives you a significance that doesn't rely on your achievements or looks. And he intends that your life, lived in his power and for his purposes, will have a positive impact on those around you (John 15:8-11).

What Is Your Dream?

When speaking at a conference about finding your passion, a woman approached me during the break. Jodi had a question.

Chapter One: Dare to Dream

"My dream is to own a flower shop," she said. "Is that a wrong thing to desire? It doesn't sound like a spiritual enough use of my time and energy. What do you think?"

I smiled, gave her a reassuring hug, and told her that God gives us our gifts and talents to use for him. Her creative gifts were part of God's image in her. He is the ultimate Creator of all that is beautiful, and for her to desire to create beauty most definitely reflected His glory.

Do you have a dream? Something you would love to do for the Lord? Something that incorporates and uses your passions and strengths? Don't push down what soars in your heart. Record here what is dancing in your mind, however impossible it seems right now.

_____

_____

_____

_____

_____

Are you too scared to dream? Be honest. No one need know. Write down what scares you about dreaming, and why.

_____

_____

_____

Go For It!

It doesn't matter how old or young you are, every stage of your life has great value.

Jesus' life-empowering statement has no age limits: *I came that you may have and enjoy life, and have it in abundance (to the full, till it overflows)* (John 10:10, AMP).

The life Jesus speaks of is spiritual, present, and eternal.

- It's a never-ending life that is yours because of faith in His death for you (Romans 6:23).

- It's a quality of life that reflects God's reality as you abide in Jesus (John 15:5).

- It's a life that has purpose and direction under the hand of God (Hebrews 12:1-2).

- It's a life that is developed by cultivating a love for God and a commitment to saying Yes to his plans for you (Philippians 2:13).

- It's a conviction about who your life belongs to; You are not your own; you were bought with a price. Therefore, honor God with your body (1 Corinthians. 6:19-20).

Do you want a fruitful life? A deeper relationship with God that also impacts others? Then allow God to direct you.

Perhaps you're wondering, "Can people like me, who are naturally scared and timid, dare to dream? Does God really have something I can do for him?" Yes, he does.

Chapter One: Dare to Dream

If God only used the naturally brave and bold, the firebrands and super-confident extroverts, many men and women who did great things would never have been called by God to act. Here are a few scared people that God not only called, but also transformed step by step:

- He told scared and resistant Moses to lead Israel out of Egypt.

- He called scared and resistant Jeremiah to be His prophet.

- He gave young, immature Joseph great dreams. Those dreams kept his heart anchored when his life turned upside down. Only later did he see God's amazing purpose for all he experienced.

Don't have a dream yet? Don't sense a call or drawing in a particular direction? Don't fret. When you're ready, God will give you a desire, a thought, a concern, or a word from others. If it involves a challenge or a new area, it may produce insecurity and fear. Pray about it. Seek God's direction. Don't let fear hold you back.

You have the amazing privilege of living a God-directed, God-empowered, and God-fulfilled life—an abundant life that touches others. Will you explore, discover, and embrace what God has for you?

Go For It!

Explore and Discover:
When I Am Old, I Want to …

Look ahead to being eighty-plus-years-old. Think about and answer the following:

When I am old, what do I want to look back on as having been an important part of my life?

_____

_____

_____

_____

When I am old, what do I want to have accomplished, experienced, or achieved with my life?

_____

_____

_____

_____

When I am old, where will I want to have invested my time, energy, and resources?

_____

_____

Chapter One: Dare to Dream

_____

_____

_____

When I am old, what kind of person do I hope to be?

_____

_____

_____

_____

_____

When I am old, what do I hope people will say about me?

_____

_____

_____

_____

_____

_All the days ordained for me were written in your
book before one of them came to be. (Psalm 139:16)_

Go For It!

Chapter Two: Review Your Life

I will remember the works of the Lord; surely I will remember your wonders of old. I will also meditate on all your work, and talk of your deeds.

Psalm 77: 10-12

Lord, Use My Life

Several years ago I was doing a Bible study that posed a question I had never thought of: "If you could ask God to do anything with your life, what would it be?"

Out of nowhere a thought came that completely shocked me. In fact, I put "Ha, Ha!" after my response. What did I write down? "Lord, I want to speak for you around the world."

It wasn't, "Lord, I want to be famous, or wealthy, or admired." I just wanted to share what I knew of the living God and his life-changing Word. But I was still horrified at myself. My immediate thoughts were, *What an egotistical thing to think. Where did such a thought come from? And who was I to desire such a thing?* Yes, for several years I taught with Bible Study Fellowship and women's groups in various churches, but what on earth could have prompted this ridiculous "around the world" idea?

Little did I know that God had planted this passion in my heart because it was his plan. The apostle Paul points to God as the instigator of all our desires to serve Him, declaring, *For God is at work within you, helping you want to obey him, and then helping you do what he wants* (Philippians 2:13, NLB).

Within two years I was asked to teach the spouses' spiritual growth program at a conference for missionary doctors and dentists, which was held alternate years in Africa and Asia. I did this for seven years. At the same time, I received an invitation to spend six weeks touring Australia as the "International Speaker" for an inter-denominational ministry.

I was unaware the organization had branches in the United Kingdom, New Zealand, and Malaysia, nor did I realize their leaders were present at the large national conference in Sydney. But God did, and invitations came from each country in the following years to speak about his reality and love.

From that one startling thought a few decades ago, I've watched with amazement and excitement as God has opened doors to minister in over twenty countries. This didn't happen because I had confidence or ambition, or was famous. It was simply God's plan.

Shaped by God to Serve Him

As I kept saying *yes* to the doors God opened, I began to see how he shapes and prepares us for serving him through our life experiences.

I was born in England, grew up spending my early childhood years in Sri Lanka, my early teens in Singapore, and my later teen years and early twenties in Kenya, East Africa. This unusual background was normal for me because my father was in the Royal Air Force and my parents loved living overseas. More recently, I also lived in Singapore for a few years with my husband.

Clearly, globetrotting is in my genes. But I didn't realize how it had shaped me for God's purposes until six weeks after the September 11, 2001, terrorist attack in New York. A friend had been asked to speak in Senegal, West Africa, at a women's missionary conference. Shortly before the event, she had to cancel for health reasons. I was asked to go in her place.

As the first session began, I looked around at the audience and saw Africans, Asians, Europeans, Canadians, and Americans. *God*, I silently prayed in awe, *You have uniquely shaped me for this. I've experienced each of these cultures. I've lived in Africa; I've lived in Asia. I come from Europe. I am an American. You have given me a passion for speaking about you, and you have made it happen for your glory.*

Travelling internationally was not something I sought or dreamed up by myself. God gave the desire and floods me with joy when I speak to people from different cultures.

As you begin to seek God's direction for your life, claim this promise he gave me long ago: *I will lead the blind by ways they have not known, along unfamiliar paths I will guide them; I will turn the darkness into light before them and make the rough places smooth* (Isaiah 42:16).

If you could do anything for God, what would it be?

_____

_____

_____

_____

_____

Go For It!

What do you think is your calling?

_____

_____

_____

_____

_____

Tracing God's hand on your life can give important clues about who you are and where he might be leading. To help you discover how God has shaped you through your background and experiences, let's begin by looking back.

Look Back: How Has God Led You?

Have you ever reflected on the path you've walked so far? Or thought about the ways God led and shaped you into the person you are now? When you wonder, or question if he will lead you in the future, look back.

How has he shaped your interests, equipped you for his plans, and directed your steps?

_____

_____

_____

_____

_____

Your Upbringing

My upbringing included living in several cultures, which prepared me for cross-cultural ministry. My parents were readers, which made me hungry to learn and read. Their marriage and parenting shaped me in many ways.

How did your upbringing influence who you are today? What impact has it had on your direction in life?

_____

_____

_____

_____

People God Has Used to Bless You

I have been blessed with a "spiritual mother" since I became a believer at age seventeen. Her strong, godly influence on me, mainly through letters from England, shaped who I have become.

Who has influenced your walk with Christ? What did they say or do that left a lasting impression?

_____

_____

_____

_____

_____

Go For It!

Books (or Other Media) That Grew Your Faith

At a time of crisis in my life, I read several books by the late J. Oswald Sanders on spiritual maturity. Another classic, J.I. Packer's *Knowing God*, deepened my understanding of God and his ways in our lives. Missionary biographies also etched into my mind that God is alive, he cares, and he acts.

What books, or other media, taught, encouraged, or inspired your faith at just the right time? How did God speak through their words to redirect your heart, your thoughts, or your decisions?

_____

_____

_____

_____

_____

Experiences of God's Presence

My decision to step away from teaching with Bible Study Fellowship was a God-led experience. So was being obedient to his call to start writing. Seeing my father become a believer at seventy was another profound experience of God's presence.

What events or experiences has God used to reveal himself to you? To direct your path in a new way? To give you a fresh vision and passion for him?

_____

_____

_____

_____

_____

Scriptures

Romans, Ephesians, Hebrews, and John's gospel are some of my favorite Bible books. As a visual learner, I also underline verses and scribble notes in the margins of my Bible. Reading these special passages brings memories of all the times where God has drawn me to him, challenged my thinking or attitude, or shown me how to handle a situation in his way, not mine.

What Bible books or verses have increased your desire for God? Can you recall the power of certain truths that touched your heart, caused you to change your direction, or increased your faith?

_____

_____

_____

_____

_____

Go For It!

As you've reflected on how God has been active in your life so far, why not take time right now to write a prayer of gratitude. You may also want to express any fears you have, or affirm your faith about the future he has for you.

_____

_____

_____

_____

_____

Look Within: How Has God Created You?

How do you respond if someone asks, "Who are you?"

Do you say, "I'm a homemaker, a teacher, a realtor, or …?"

Have you ever realized this answer is not *who* you are, it is what you do?

To know who you are requires you to:

- Discover your passions.

- Analyze your strengths.

- Look at your proven abilities.

- Acknowledge your inherent talents.

- Identify the spiritual gifts you've received to serve and build up others.

Chapter Two: Review Your Life

Here are some questions to help you learn more about yourself.

In what environment do I function best? Do I prefer structure and stated expectations? Or do I need freedom to take the initiative?

_____

_____

_____

_____

_____

In what areas do people praise and appreciate me? What do they comment on? Is this a frequent response?

_____

_____

_____

_____

_____

What gets me up in the morning with a sense of anticipation?

_____

_____

_____

Go For It!

_____

_____

What activity or involvement gives me energy?

_____

_____

_____

_____

How would a close friend or spouse describe my strengths and passion?

_____

_____

_____

_____

As you explore how God has made you, try asking yourself a different kind of question:

_____

_____

_____

_____

_____

What have I done that I'd NEVER do again?

_____

_____

_____

_____

Now probe a little deeper and ask yourself WHY you feel that way:

What didn't you enjoy about the experience?

_____

_____

_____

_____

_____

Were there expectations you had, or others had, that contributed to your discomfort?

_____

_____

Go For It!

_____

_____

_____

What did you learn about yourself from the experience that can guide you in the future?

_____

_____

_____

_____

_____

Hi! I'm the Hospital Chaplain.

Some years ago, I had an opportunity to volunteer as a hospital chaplain and thought it would be a wonderful way to serve the Lord. Plus, it was in the hospital where my husband worked. What could be better?

I envisioned myself being a modern day Florence Nightingale (the British founder of the nursing profession), comforting women in pain, and easing their anxiety. I saw myself knocking on a patient's door, being graciously received, and laying my cool hand on their fevered brow as I prayed for them. While indulging my dramatic imagination, it never occurred to me this was anything other than a divine appointment to serve the Lord.

Once my brief training was over, I made rounds by myself. Instead of warm, fuzzy feelings and glowing with the joy of serving the sick in Jesus' name, I began to dread going to the hospital. I didn't have a clue what I was doing and quickly recognized this ministry was not for me.

I felt I was intruding on the women I visited and convinced myself they probably wished I would go away. After all, I reasoned, if I were lying in my hospital bed moaning in pain, without a shred of make-up hiding my blotchy face, would I want to be seen by a complete stranger? No. I would not. Three months later, my initial commitment fulfilled, I eagerly resigned.

In my saner moments, I recognized that a lot of my feelings did not reflect reality. My well-intentioned ministry wasn't a complete fiasco, and there were women who welcomed my visits.

One elderly woman, whose brother was terminally ill, asked me to sit with her during a medical conference regarding his treatment. This was a privilege. So was coming alongside mothers sitting with their desperately ill children in the pediatric intensive care ward. But would I volunteer again? Never.

When I told a friend that I wouldn't be continuing after my three-month commitment, she offered to interview for the position. A trained nurse with a counseling degree, she knew what she was doing, loved caring for the sick, and stayed for years.

Even though I made a mistake in volunteering as a hospital chaplain, I did learn some things about following God's leading that made the experience valuable. Let me share them with you, courtesy of my impulsive nature.

Go For It!

Any time a new opportunity comes:

- Stop and think carefully about what will be expected of you. Ask questions and listen.

- Probe yourself gently but honestly. Are you suited by experience, temperament, or God-given desire for this new experience? What attracts you to it?

- Gather input from those who love you, know your gifts, and will be honest.

- Pray longer and more seriously before volunteering for something you know little about.

Failure is a Path to Discovery

Have you had a job, volunteer involvement, or been part of a ministry that didn't turn out as you hoped? Instead of feeling a failure, look at it as a learning experience.

What useful information have you learned about yourself from these kinds of situations?

_____

_____

_____

_____

Chapter Two: Review Your Life

God Chose Your Gifts

The Bible makes it clear that God has chosen, loved and gifted each believer with both human strengths and spiritual gifts.

In a story that greatly influences my life choices, Jesus told about a man who entrusted his property to three servants. He gave them different amounts of money (talents) and expected them to invest it for him.

Two of the servants did something with what they were given, and the owner was very pleased. But one of the servants decided to bury his talent. He did nothing with it. And the owner was not happy (Matthew 25:14-30).

The talents described in Scripture symbolize the gifts and abilities God has given us. We don't all receive the same capabilities or have the same spiritual strengths. But all of us are accountable to use what we've been given.

What Are Your Gifts?

Identifying your spiritual gifts is an important part of sensing how God is leading you. Not everyone is called to be a leader, teach, cook meals or cuddle babies in the nursery. God has given a huge variety of gifts to meet the different needs within the Body of Christ and in the wider world.

Where Do You Say Your Gifts and Interests Lie?

_____

_____

_____

Go For It!

_____

_____

Where Have You Used Them?

_____

_____

_____

_____

_____

Now look back at times when you've used the talents God has given you. Did people affirm you? Did you feel joy, a sense of doing what fits you? Those are good indicators you're doing what God has gifted you to do.

If you're not familiar with what the Bible teaches on spiritual gifts, let me encourage you to take half an hour, find a quiet place to read, and think about what God is saying to you in 1 Corinthians 12 and Romans 12: 3-8.

God Uses Your Personality

Being aware of your personality strengths and needs is also a vital part of making good choices.

In reviewing your life so far, which of the following sounds most like you?

- You're an achiever. You have a vision and an internal fire to accomplish more, to lead others, to make things happen.

- You're an organizer. Your inner drive pushes you to create structure, order, and logical plans to achieve the best outcome.

- You're a connector. Your passion is to pull people together, build bridges, and network.

- You're an idea person. Your creativity flows in every situation.

It takes time to review your past experiences and discover where to invest your energy in the days ahead. Here are some questions that will help you analyze where you function best.

Do I thrive on working with people or working alone? Or do I need a mix of stimulating activities plus times of quiet to be re-energized?

_____

_____

_____

_____

_____

Do I prefer taking risks rather than staying in a safe routine? What bores me? What excites me?

_____

_____

_____

Go For It!

_____

_____

Do I enjoy taking a leadership role or would I rather be a follower?

_____

_____

_____

_____

_____

How do you describe your personality?

_____

_____

_____

_____

How does your personality affect what you enjoy doing?

_____

_____

_____

Chapter Two: Review Your Life

You're a unique combination of genetics, family background, life experiences, personality, and spiritual gifts plus many other factors. Because of this, how you express your God-created strengths will vary.

Think of yourself as a detective searching for information about *you*. The more you find, the better you'll be at evaluating whether a new path or involvement is what God has shaped you for.

Go For It!

Explore and Discover:
Who Am I?

Be willing to take the time needed to review your past experiences. Reflecting is a valuable tool for finding out how God has put you together and shaped you for His purposes.

To summarize what you've learned, let me encourage you to do these simple exercises.

List five things you love to do.

- Put a mark beside each one:
- A for alone. P for with people. AP— for both.
- Then number your most enjoyable activities, with 5 being the highest.

1. _____

_____

_____

2. _____

_____

_____

3. _____

_____

_____

4. _____

  _____

  _____

5. _____

  _____

  _____

Record five skills that you have.

- Place a * next to the skills you most enjoy.
- Place a + next to the skills you're most proficient at.
- Number the skills that are most important to you. Think about why.

1. _____

  _____

  _____

2. _____

  _____

  _____

3. _____

  _____

  _____

Go For It!

4. _____

_____

_____

5. _____

_____

_____

Reflect on the information you gathered using the following as a guide.

- I learned _____

_____

- I realized _____

_____

- I was surprised _____

_____

- I was pleased _____

_____

You've reviewed your life and discovered more about yourself and how God has shaped you. Now, how do you answer the question, "Who are you?"

_____

_____

_____

_____

_____

Whatever you do, work at it with all your heart, as working for the Lord, not for men. (Colossians 3:23)

Go For It!

Chapter Three: Explore Opportunities

It is God who works in you to will and to act according to his good purpose.

Philippians 2:13

After identifying some of your passions and strengths, the next step is to explore where these can be part of your life.

If your passion is caring for people, consider the many paths open to you: working with the elderly; with children in the foster care system; with pregnant or homeless teens; victims of domestic violence or human trafficking; ex-prisoners—the list is endless.

You might want to mentor, lead a study for singles, organize events, teach, or administrate. Whether you're considering a paying job or a volunteer position, think about who you are, and what grabs your heart.

To help you clarify this next step, how would you answer the following?

- The ideal organization or activity I'd like to be involved with is:

_____

_____

_____

Go For It!

_____

_____

- The skills I'd like to use are:

_____

_____

_____

_____

_____

- The tasks I'd enjoy are:

_____

_____

_____

_____

_____

- My friends say they see these strengths and gifts in me:

_____

_____

_____

_____

_____

Chapter Three: Explore Opportunities

What Makes You Come Alive?

Decide to go for it and you'll inevitably step out of the familiar into an experience that stretches your faith. It can also stretch your mind.

Go For Your Dream

I had dreamed of getting a Masters in counseling for a long time. After exploring several programs, it became clear; unless I wanted to enroll as an undergraduate student, I wouldn't be accepted. Why? Because an undergraduate degree was required by Oregon law.

Unfortunately, I lived nowhere near a college during the years most young people attended school. I lived in Nairobi, Kenya, supporting myself from the age of seventeen to twenty-two, when I got married and came to America. I took some classes at the University of Iowa in the early years and loved them, but then chose to stay home full-time with my two little ones. The result? I never graduated from college.

At midlife, after teaching with Bible Study Fellowship for seven years and in local churches for another four, I began speaking at retreats and conferences. I also wrote books and Bible studies. With an active ministry, leaving everything to go to college for four years didn't make sense.

I thought my dream of going to graduate school could never happen. But it did. Instead of getting a counseling degree, the door opened at a local seminary to get a Masters in Spiritual Formation and Direction. Not only did I grow in helping others develop their walk with God, but I also grew in understanding myself.

Go For It!

Do you have a longing that you've put on the shelf? Perhaps a dream from when you were a child? Take a few moments to sit quietly and see what bubbles up from the recesses of your heart, then jot it down.

_____

_____

_____

_____

_____

You have completed step one, which is recognizing a desire implanted long ago. Step two is exploring how that desire can be experienced now and in the future

Past Dreams—Present Opportunities

My friend and long-term ministry assistant, Karen, is a Special Education teacher. As a child, she met many missionaries and dreamed of becoming one herself. Her heart was set on Africa. As life took over, her childhood desire became a distant memory. But God hadn't forgotten the dream he gave her.

Now in her sixties, energetic, and overflowing with passion, Karen has made several trips to Kenya. Using all she has learned over the years, she has taught hundreds of national teachers how to respond to children with special needs. By also educating their parents, she gave them desperately needed hope as well as practical ways to help their children in a resource-limited country.

In addition to going to Kenya, God has expanded Karen's dream with travels to former Soviet countries to teach and encourage.

Chapter Three: Explore Opportunities

If you have been waiting for years, or even decades, to see a dream become reality, don't give up hope. Explore what opportunities exist, watching for God's hand. He still answers prayer and delights to fulfill the desires he placed in your heart, even if his answers come in unexpected ways.

Six Key Questions When Facing Crossroads

Acting on your D.R.E.A.M. requires prayer and thought, as well as checking to see if it fits with God's path for you. As you start exploring opportunities, here are six key questions to ask yourself:

1. **Will this path increase my love for God or draw me away?**

2. **Does this choice reflect my reputation as a follower of Christ?**

3. **Would a spiritually mature friend agree with this decision?**

4. **Is this choice pleasing to the heart of God?**

5. **Will this choice deepen God's work in me?**

6. **As I envision offering this plan to God, do I feel at peace or uneasy?**

Scripture is full of guidance about making God-honoring decisions. Here's just one passage full of powerful principles for today, given by the prophet Jeremiah to Israel.

This is what the Lord says: *"Stand at the crossroads and look; ask for the ancient paths, ask where the good way is, and walk in it, and you will find rest for your souls."* (Jeremiah 6:16)

Go For It!

Let's look at the details of what God said, but first let's define crossroads.

Crossroads. These are places where your decision could change the direction of your life and shape who you become. Everyone faces external crossroads that affect where we live and what we do. But we also face internal crossroads, moments when our values, moral character, and priorities are tested, resulting in consequences that could be either positive or negative. God's words to Israel and to us is the same: be wise when you're standing at life-impacting crossroads.

Stand. Be still. Stop. Don't race through the choices facing you. Ask yourself: Will making this choice cause me to drift from God, or will it draw me closer?

Look. Evaluate the short and long term ramifications, not just for you but also for others affected by your choice.

Ask. Use the six questions above to help you find God's path. Ask for spiritual wisdom to discern if you're being driven by your emotions, hidden longings, or fears. Emotions by themselves are not indicators of God's will. God has given you a mind to think, and his Word to meet your need for clear direction. Use all the avenues he has provided. (Proverbs 3:5-8)

If you realize your choice wasn't wise, remember it is never too late to turn around. You can go back. You can begin again. Poor decisions do *not* have to keep you stuck forever.

Do what God says: Stand, look carefully; ask him which way to go. Then walk in obedience to His leading.

Say Yes To God—Let Yourself Be Stretched

When I left teaching with Bible Study Fellowship, I did something I'd never considered before. Even though I had no personal exposure to domestic violence, as soon as I saw an appeal for volunteers to help in a women's shelter, I knew it was something I wanted to do.

At first, my weekly tasks included checking on the number of beds available in the city where I live. Most days all the shelters were full. Women were desperate to find a safe place for themselves and their children. Telling them nothing was available was heartbreaking.

During my shifts, I answered the phone, helped with the clothes closet, and played with the children—some of whom were so traumatized they screamed in fear when anyone came close. Later, I facilitated a support group for women who were ordered by the court to get help. Hearing their raw stories of longing for love, but instead receiving verbal abuse, threats, and beatings, left me shaken.

From knowing nothing about this very real issue in our culture (and in most cultures), I gained an education that has proven invaluable. Whether I'm talking privately to a woman about her abusive marriage or teaching on this topic from a Biblical perspective, I'm thankful God nudged me to get involved.

What has been the outcome since I stepped into such an unfamiliar world?

1. **I've listened to many women's stories, giving comfort and counsel.**

2. **I've grown in my awareness of how widespread this problem is.**

3. I've taught on God's love for women and his hatred of abuse.

4. I've learned how to advise women if they need to leave for their own safety.

5. I've been blessed to speak to both singles and marrieds about 'red flags' to watch for in their relationships—and what to do about them.

As you seek wisdom about where to serve God and others, ask yourself:

- What inspires me? Stirs my heart? Moves me to want to do something for the Lord?

- Will this new step use my talents, expand my horizons, and cause me to grow?

- Am I willing to risk and break through fears and stereotypes that hold me back?

Explore and Discover:
What Tugs at Your Heart?

After the disappearance of the Malaysian Airlines flight, which went missing on its way from Kuala Lumpur to Beijing, my thoughts went back to a group of widows I had spoken to recently in Singapore.

I had expected the group to be mainly older ladies who had lost their husbands after many years together. That wasn't the case. These precious widows spanned every age. They had lost their spouses through different illnesses and various kinds of accidents including a plane crash. The founder of the group shared her story with me.

This caring ministry began after the unexpected death of her husband. A friend invited her to church, and following some special experiences with the Lord, she became a Christian. God then gave her a desire to help other women dealing with the shock, loss, and adjustment of widowhood. Her organization now reaches out to Singaporean widows of all ages and beliefs.

As you consider how God might use your life experiences to help others, let me give you a brief list of possibilities. You can add your own.

Have You:

- Lost a family member or close friend to death?

- Lost a child to drugs, alcohol, or other addictions?

- A child with special needs?

- Lost a child in a child-custody suit?

Go For It!

- Experienced an abortion?

- Experienced domestic violence or abuse as a child?

- Experienced divorce or abandonment?

- Been financially devastated?

- Been a single parent?

- Unemployed?

- Felt friendless and unwanted?

- Other difficult life experiences?

Ask Yourself:

- How did (does) God help me?

- How did (does) he give me courage, comfort, help, and healing?

- What practical ways to cope has he shown me?

Apply What You've Learned. Ask Yourself:

- How can I reach out to other women experiencing what I have?

Could I send a note or email? Give a hug? Stop to give time and a listening ear? Give a small gift? Take her out for coffee or a meal? Invite her to a supportive group?

- Am I using what I've learned through my life to help others, or am I letting it go to waste?

Chapter Three: Explore Opportunities

Two women, one a widow in her early forties and the other a divorcée, started a group in their church for single women. Their combined life experiences of loss, change, and the challenges of a new path prompted them to reach out. God gave them the desire, whispered, "go for it," and is now making them a blessing.

What needs and opportunities do you see around you? Where might God want you to step in?

_____

_____

_____

_____

_____

Faith by itself, if it is not accompanied by action, is dead. (James 2: 17)

Go For It!

Chapter Four: Anticipate Obstacles

Let us run with perseverance the race
marked out for us.

Hebrews 12:1b

Obstacles Are Inevitable

Life is full of obstacles, but we belong to the Obstacle Solver, the Obstacle Remover, and the One who calls us forward to faith and confidence in him. There are no smooth paths as we follow God's purposes for our lives, and no dream happens without difficulties.

Two hundred years ago, William Lloyd Garrison grew up believing that slavery was a detestable offense against God and humanity. He dreamed what must have seemed an impossible dream: one day, slavery would be eliminated from America.

In England, William Wilberforce had the same dream. Both Garrison and Wilberforce faced hostility and condemnation for their convictions, but their commitment inspired others to share their passion. Ultimately, this seemingly impossible dream was accomplished. Did they face obstacles? Absolutely.

More recently Adrianne Haslet-Davis, a professional ballroom dancer lost her lower leg in the Boston Marathon bombing. She later performed at a TED conference in Vancouver, Canada, and participated in Dancing with the Stars. Did she have to overcome pain, physical setbacks, and battle discouragement as she worked to accomplish her dream? Of course.

The same is true when God gives you a dream.

Here's a reality check: Any time you dream about doing something new, have a God-given restless desire for more, or know something must change, you *will* face obstacles. This is nothing new.

Struggles and disappointments happen. They are ways God shapes and strengthens your faith, purifies your longing, and develops a perseverance that keeps you running the race set before you (Hebrews 12:1-3). Scripture is full of instruction and inspiring examples about what to expect when we follow God's call. Here are a few. Notice what it took:

- Exodus 3-4: Moses was called to command Pharaoh to let God's people go, but it didn't happen quickly or easily. It took constant dependence on God, listening, and patient persistence.

- Joshua 1: Joshua was told to lead the Israelites into the Promised Land after Moses died. Success ultimately came because Joshua checked every step with God's Word and was careful to do everything in it. It took constant courage, determination, and unwavering focus on God's promises.

- Ruth 1: When Ruth had the opportunity to go back to all that was familiar, she chose instead to risk and step into the unknown. Her choice required a constant commitment, trust, and belief in God's loving care. It's the same for you and me.

Chapter Four: Anticipate Obstacles

Drawing us to something new, God implants the desire and gives the courage to step forward. The future is always unknown to us, but not to him.

The presence of obstacles does not mean God is saying no to your dream. Moses, Joshua, Ruth, and many others encountered numerous discouragements, but they overcame them by their real trust in a very real God.

Master Your Fear

Do you believe God has laid a dream, a longing, or a direction on your heart? But your mind is filled with panicky thoughts of "what if," "how will I cope," and "I can't do that." "God, please don't ask me."

Fear is one of our greatest barriers to moving forward. Whether it's a new relationship, job, ministry, or action that stretches and takes you beyond your comfort zone, fear hovers. But it only has the power to control and rob you of what God desires for your life if you let it.

In his challenging book, *The Dream Releasers*, author and pastor Wayne Cordeiro writes about visiting cemeteries and wondering about the unrealized dreams of those buried there.[2] He speculates about the unwritten poems, books, music, unattained success, unfulfilled promise, and lives that fell short of God's intended purpose.

You and I are not in the grave yet. Nor do we have to stay in a rut, as comfortable as that can be. God calls us to press on. To do this requires we master our fears about stepping into the unknown when God calls.

---

2   Wayne Cordeiro, *The Dream Releasers*. (Ventura, CA: Regal Books, 2002), 61-62.

Go For It!

Let me ask you, have you ever examined your fear and looked at where it comes from? Fear might be triggered by past experiences, but most often it comes from our focus. As followers of Jesus, we have a choice: We can live under the burden of fear, or we can focus on, claim, and apply the resources God gives.

To Break Free from Fear-focused Thinking, Take Action:

1. **Refocus your mind on God's infinite power at work in you, not your own finite capabilities (Ephesians 3:20).**

2. **Rehearse, reaffirm, and rejoice in who God is and what he has promised: He is in control of this world. He is in control of your life. He will work all things together for your ultimate good (Psalms 27:1, 8; 28: 6-7).**

3. **Rephrase the words you speak to yourself. Refuse to reinforce your doubts and fears. Instead, train yourself to say strongly and confidently:** *I trust in you, O Lord. I say You are my God. My times are in Your hands* **(Psalm 31:4-15).**

4. **Review your emotions. Refuse to allow fear and anxiety to rule your emotions. God promises you peace when you choose to trust him (Philippians 4:6-7).**

5. **Reach out. When you need help, Jesus invites you to:**

   - Come to his throne of grace

   - Come with confidence

   - *Come and receive grace, mercy, and help in your time of need* (Hebrews 4:16).

Chapter Four: Anticipate Obstacles

Being a natural wimp I frequently cling to a God-given, perspective-changing promise found in Isaiah 26:3, *You will keep him in perfect peace, whose mind is stayed on you, because he trusts in you.*

How about you? What do you keep your mind on? You and your weaknessess or God and his promises?

Overcome Your Self-Talk Traps

Many dreams die before they ever get started. Do you know why? Because we talk ourselves out of stepping forward into the unknown.

Here are eight common self-talk traps, which can hold you back. You tell yourself:

1. **To dream is foolish. It's a crazy idea for someone like me.**

2. **Who am I to attempt something new and challenging?**

3. **Why risk looking foolish?**

4. **It's just a waste of time and money.**

5. **My family will be put out. It will shake up our routine.**

6. **I was told I'd never amount to much, so why try?**

7. **I'm not needed, and I have nothing to contribute.**

8. **Just be content. Settle for what is. Forget your desires and stirrings.**

There are many more thoughts and phrases that we allow to destroy our God-given dreams. **Which ones do you wrestle with?**

Go For It!

_____

_____

_____

_____

_____

To free yourself, question your self-talk.

- Don't roll over and play dead when you're bullied and assaulted by your negative inner critic. What you tell yourself is often not true. Nor is it coming from the Holy Spirit. Knowing the truth about yourself and who you are in Christ brings freedom.

  Jesus promised, If you hold to my teachings you are really my disciples. Then you will know the truth, and the truth will set you free (John 8:32).

- Fight back by questioning the statements you hear. Are they true? Or are they lies you've absorbed without question? Are they unproven assumptions you've made about yourself because someone else said that to you? Are they springing from fears, or lies you need to pray about and refute with God's Word?

  We demolish arguments and every pretension that sets itself up against the knowledge of God, and we take captive every thought to make it obedient to Christ (2 Corinthians 10:5).

To free yourself from unbiblical self-talk, look at how God has, and is, moving in your mind and heart. If you're open to him, life can be full of new, stimulating, and stretching challenges. He promises to make a way, providing all you need to grow and flourish.

> *See, I am doing a new thing! Now it springs up; do you not perceive it? I am making a way in the desert and streams in the wasteland.* (Isaiah 43:19)

Where has God stirred you to step forward before? Can you recall two or three occasions where you did something new because you felt God's nudge? Make a note of these below.

_____

_____

_____

_____

Take a moment to think more deeply about the events you just listed. How did they bless you and make you a blessing to others?

_____

_____

_____

_____

When your mind is filled with fears of various kinds, speak truth to yourself. Repeat these foundational facts of faith until they become your automatic response to fearful thoughts:

- God is at work in me.

- God is for me.

- God will provide all I need.

- God's purpose is to mature my faith, deepen my trust, and expand my experience of him.

- God is transforming me into the likeness of Jesus, who always did what pleased him.

With this truthful, faith-building self-talk, you'll find yourself confidently saying *yes* to what God has for you.

Break Through Money Barriers

When you're wondering how to finance your dream or get started with a class or online program, finding the money is often a big obstacle.

Even though *the love of money is a root of all kinds of evil* (1 Timothy 6:10), needing money and using it wisely is not the same as loving it. We need money for life's necessities and many times we also need it to make our God-given dreams a reality. So what's the answer?

1. Ask God to provide wisdom and direction.

Let me encourage you to take a moment and do that by writing a prayer. Tell God your needs, expressing your trust that he will guide and provide.

_____

_____

_____

_____

_____

2. Get practical. List where your money usually goes.

_____

_____

_____

_____

What different financial choices can you make?

_____

_____

_____

_____

_____

Go For It!

What do small indulgences cost you each month? Which can you give up to meet your greater goal?

_____

_____

_____

_____

_____

Where else could you cut back to reduce monthly spending?

_____

_____

_____

_____

_____

What amount do you actually need to take the next step?

_____

_____

_____

_____

_____

Can you move toward your goal with less than your ideal amount?

_____

_____

_____

_____

_____

3. Assess your priorities.

Which is most important to you? Spending as usual, or adjusting your spending as necessary? Think realistically about the likely outcomes of each choice.

_____

_____

_____

_____

_____

4. Approach others.

Your dream might stir such passion and urgency in you that God leads you to share it with others. If this is the case, pray that people will share your vision and join you. Go for it and ask for support.

Go For It!

Seek Family Harmony

Children are not necessarily obstacles to experiencing your dreams. But taking care of them must come first. During those years when your children need loving attention, their physical, spiritual, psychological, and emotional needs must be primary. Other God-given and God-honoring priorities are being a help and support to your husband, elderly parents, or close family members.

Does this mean your dreams and nudges from God must be abandoned? Or can you find ways to negotiate, compromise, and find space in your life to go for it?

Let me encourage you to be realistic when sharing your dreams and hopes with your family, and even with certain friends. Some will be excited for you and cheer you on. But some won't. Here's why:

- Changes in your schedule, priorities, and availability will likely affect them.

- Everyone likes their lives to go along smoothly and not have fresh demands placed on them.

- Family members and others who tend toward negativity could be hurtful when you share your vision.

- Some will urge you to keep things as they are and not take a risk or challenge, perhaps fearing you will grow away from them.

Whatever the response you face, remember *You are God's workmanship, created in Christ Jesus to do good works, which God prepared in advance for you to do* (Ephesians 2:10).

Keep your eyes open to God working on your behalf. Refuse to let the discouragers defeat you. Instead, look for those divine encounters, people God will send across your path to affirm and support your dream. Why do they encourage you? Because they recognize his hand on your life and that he is at work in you.

Time Can Be Stretched

One of the most common barriers we face is a lack of time. Few of us have enough space in our lives to do everything we're drawn to, but we do have enough time to do what God has planned for us.

To follow the dreams and desires God put within you takes not only thought and prayer but also persistence. As you cling to the fact that God's wisdom and direction are available, look for ways to overcome what's blocking your path. Think about what the apostle James promised and act on it, *If any of you lack wisdom, he should ask God who gives generously to all without finding fault, and it will be given to him* (James 1:5).

Here are four strategies to get beyond wasting the time you do have and kick-start your dream.

1. **Consider what you need to do. What specific steps are needed to make immediate progress? Make lists. Prioritize them, and begin.**

_____

_____

_____

Go For It!

_____

_____

2. **Check your schedule. Daily, weekly, monthly. Where can you fit in the time needed to prepare or carry out your dream? What can you eliminate to make time for a class, an online course, or participating in an activity that touches your heart?**

_____

_____

_____

_____

_____

3. **Choose your priorities. Give yourself permission to change priorities with different seasons of life. If God is calling you to something new, what might have to be eliminated? Pray for insight into possibly reshaping a long-standing (but not divinely ordained) schedule or assumptions about what you should be doing. (For more help, work through chapters 9 and 10 in my book** _I'm Too Young to Be This Old._**)**[3]

_____

_____

_____

---

3   Poppy Smith, _I'm Too Young to Be This Old._ (Eugene, OR: Harvest House Publishers, 1997), 17-18.

_____

_____

4. Count progress in small steps. To accomplish even small steps each week is progress. Waiting until you have large chunks of time can be self-defeating. What can you do today or this week?

_____

_____

_____

_____

_____

Go For It!

Explore and Discover:
What Are My Personal Obstacles?
What Are the Solutions?

Personal Obstacles:

_____

_____

_____

_____

List all the steps needed to implement possible solutions:

_____

_____

_____

_____

Schedule each step on your calendar, (not a scrap of paper as I have a tendency to do).

Now go do it! Check off each step, item by item. It's a great way to feel good and be motivated to keep going.

*Be very careful then, how you live—not as unwise
but as wise, making the most of every opportunity.*
(Ephesians 5:15-16a)

Chapter Five: Move Forward

Fan into flame the gift of God which is in you.

2 Timothy 1:6

Stomp on Dream Killers

One of the hardest battles we face when dealing with a God-given dream or longing is comparison. It's easy to think that other people have what we don't. More talent, more money, more confidence, more spiritual gifts, more connections, more, more, more.

A devotion from *Streams in the Desert* beautifully illustrates our problem with comparisons.[4]

A gardener looked at his plants one day. They were all withered and dying. He wanted to know the problem, so he asked the oak tree what the problem was. The oak tree responded, 'I'm tired of life, and I might as well die because I'm not as beautiful as the other trees. I have thick limbs, and I wish I were like those slim and lovely pine trees.'

When he asked the pine tree what was wrong, the pine answered he was miserable because he couldn't bear grapes like the grapevine.

The grapevine said he was unhappy and might as well throw away his life because the fruit he produced was so small. He

---

4   L.B.Cowman, *Streams in the Desert.* Edited by James Reimann. *(Grand Rapids, MI, Zondervan, 1997).* January 7.

couldn't stand erect and produce fruit the size of peaches so what good was he.

He asked the geranium why he was withering and discovered he was fretting because he wasn't tall and fragrant like the lilac.

Wherever he went in the garden, the gardener got the same unhappy responses —until he came to the violet. Finding the violet's face bright and happy he said,

'Well, violet, I'm glad to find one brave little flower in the middle of this discouragement. You don't seem to be the least unhappy about who you are.' The violet answered, 'No, I'm not unhappy with myself. I know I'm small, but I also realize that if you had wanted me to be like the oak or pine or peach tree or even a lilac, you would have planted one. Because I know you wanted a violet, I'm determined to be the best little violet I can be.'

Which plant do you resonate with? Why?

_____

_____

_____

_____

_____

How do the words "I'm determined to be the best I can be" challenge you?

_____

_____

Chapter Five: Move Forward

_____

_____

_____

Learn from the violet.

The violet recognized the many differences between her and the other plants. But, instead of focusing on what she wasn't, she focused on knowing the gardener wanted her exactly as she was. The small, pretty violet was content, she was happy, and she delighted in bringing beauty and fragrance to the place she was planted.

How can you be content? Recognize and cherish who you are.

No matter how God uses others, you are a woman of value to him, your family, and yourself. If you doubt that, spend some time thinking about Christ's death on the cross for you. It is the deepest proof of your value to God.

To spend time questioning your value is to accept another of Satan's schemes to discourage and keep you from living a faith-filled and joy-filled life. Instead, intentionally accept with wonder and gratitude that you _are_ God's uniquely created and beloved daughter.

Train your mind to believe truth rather than a lie by reminding yourself of your uniqueness. To do this, take time to list the following.

(Now's your chance to forget modesty and be bold. Describe yourself with positive and truthful statements. After all, you are a daughter of the King.)

Go For It!

My Gifts:

_____

_____

_____

_____

_____

My talents, strengths, good points:

_____

_____

_____

_____

_____

My special experiences of God's presence:

_____

_____

_____

_____

_____

Chapter Five: Move Forward

Instead of focusing on what kills your dreams, keep focusing on the One who gives you your dreams. He promises he will work in you so claim this truth and apply it to yourself.

Now to him who is able to do immeasurably
more than all we ask or imagine, according to
the power that is work within us, to him be glory
in the church and in Christ Jesus throughout all
generations. (Ephesians 3:20)

Trust God—Grow Your Faith

I'm a natural scaredy cat. I don't like heights, or depths, or the unknown. But there are times when I have sensed God drawing me into something totally new—and it's always something I don't feel remotely capable of doing.

Apart from the few super-confident, let-me-at-it types, many of us find the familiar more comfortable. However, the familiar can become a rut, which keeps you from personal growth and deprives you of experiencing God's reality in new and amazing ways.

Should I Do This—or That?

After teaching my Bible Study Fellowship class for seven years, I began to feel restless, which can sometimes be a sign that God is getting you ready for a new move or expansion of your life. Thoughts of stepping down from my position became a steady drumbeat. Should I, or shouldn't I?

Was God moving me out of teaching my class? Did he have something else in mind? I didn't know. What I did know was I couldn't ignore my inner wrestling. Finally, I made a list of pros and cons. One of the strongest pros for stepping down was being available if my parents, who lived in England, needed me.

Go For It!

Feelings Are Not an Infallible Guide.

Feelings, on their own, are definitely not a sure-fire way to know whether to stay where we are or to move forward. Unfortunately, I've seen too many foolish and ultimately heart-breaking decisions made under the powerful pull of unexamined emotions.

We know that feelings are a rich part of our lives. They are God-given. But life-changing decisions driven by feelings need checking with Scripture, the input of wise and mature friends, and an awareness that God is leading you.

When I was grappling with whether to leave for what was an unknown future, a Scripture I hadn't noticed before grabbed my attention. I sensed the Lord was making a statement to me, even a promise. In speaking to Martha at the grave of Lazarus, Jesus said: *Did I not tell you that if you believed, you would see the glory of God?* (John 11:40).

I had no idea what this meant; I only knew God's Spirit was telling me to trust him for what lay beyond the familiar.

A few months after I resigned, my father called from England. My mother was hospitalized with a heart attack and not expected to live. His trembling voice asking if I could come right away brought me to tears.

Earlier in the year, this possible scenario had constantly played in my mind. Now it had happened. Having followed the inner urging of the Holy Spirit to trust God for what lay ahead, I was free to leave immediately and be with my mother as she slipped away.

A week later my seventy-year-old father came to Christ. God had orchestrated what happened six months earlier, impressing on me to step out of the familiar and into a future known only to him.

Chapter Five: Move Forward

Leaving Bible Study Fellowship, where I was stretched and blessed every week for twelve years, allowed God to begin the next chapter in my life. In his plan, a much wider sphere of speaking, writing books, and encouraging others began. Today I look back in amazement and awe.

I don't know if God is calling you to move into something new or not. But if he is, be willing to say *yes* and step into the adventure he has for you.

My friend Carole's inspiring story is found in my book, *I'm Too Young to Be This Old*:[5]

Carole dreamed of finishing her degree and becoming a counselor. However, she had an unemployed husband who struggled with depression plus three children to support. Being realistic, she knew it wasn't going to be easy to accomplish her goal. But instead of giving up, she enrolled in a local college taking one class at a time. While working a day job, she eventually achieved her undergraduate degree.

After finding employment as an aide at her local school, Carole discovered that the school district would pay for certain staff to get their master's degree while working for them. It wasn't the exact field she dreamed of, but it enabled her to get the higher education she wanted.

Talking with Carole a few years later, she commented, "I wanted to be a counselor, but in the job I now have working with special needs children, I get to do a lot of listening and counseling with the parents of my students. It wasn't exactly the path I'd planned, but God *has* fulfilled the desire of my heart to counsel and help others."

---

5   Poppy Smith, *I'm Too Young to Be This Old.* (Eugene, OR: Harvest House Publishers, 1997), *51, 137.*

Go For It!

Carole pursued her dream even though her circumstances were less than ideal. She prayed, was flexible, and took one step, then another. As a result of moving forward, of saying yes to the nudges of the Holy Spirit, her world expanded, filling her with the joy that comes from living a life that honors God.

You've heard some of my story. In chapter three, I gave you a glimpse into how God is using Karen globally to share her knowledge about children with special needs. And you've read about Carol's longings and how God creatively led her into work she loves.

Think about your own story. What is it? And what more do you dream God might have for you—whatever your age?

_____

_____

_____

_____

_____

What Are You Waiting For?

We all want to hear the thrilling words, *Well done, good and faithful servant! You have been faithful with a few things. I will put you in charge of many things* (Matthew 25:14-30).

Yes, it can be scary. It can be complicated. But your courage to move forward also brings huge benefits. Who benefits from your courage, trust, and faith?

Chapter Five: Move Forward

- You do. You will see you are far more capable than what you might have thought. You will experience God's real presence and amazing answers to prayer. You'll see him make you into someone you might never have become if you shrink back from his invitation to go for it.

- Others do. Wherever your new steps lead you, if God is leading, others will be blessed.

- God is pleased. He created you with abilities. He blessed you with strengths, talents, gifts, education, and countless other good things, and he calls you to go for it. You were created for something far greater than an easy life. You were created to make your life count for him and his kingdom.

So let me ask you one last question:

What Is Holding You Back from Moving Forward?

- The right person to come along?

- The children to grow up?

- Somebody to take care of you?

- To finish your education?

- Someone to notice your plight?

- Someone to offer you a job?

- Your financial problems to end?

- Something bad to happen?

- Someone else to change?

Go For It!

- Someone else to make the decision?

- Someone to discover you?

- What else?

Explore and Discover:
Take One Small Step

You've heard the saying, "Every journey begins with one small step." It's true. Without taking one small step, God-given passions fizzle and die. Sadly, you might look back later and realize:

- I never pursued what God put on my heart.

- I never sought greater horizons—something new, stretching, and out of my comfort zone.

- I never acted on my dreams, overcame obstacles, or saw what God could do.

- I never tasted the fulfillment of my dreams, joyfully discovering what he had for me.

If God has called you to step into something new, or given you a passion or dream, don't let time drift by before taking one small step.

What step can you take this week? Here are some suggestions:

- Go online and research your area of interest. Type in several keywords and educate yourself.

- Go to websites, read relevant blogs and articles.

- Check classes available for training —community colleges, universities, online sites.

- Offer to help, ask to observe, visit with someone who does what interests you.

- Volunteer and discover if the dream you have meets with your reality.

- Look for a positive, faith-filled friend to encourage you. A buddy can support, inspire, help you evaluate your path, and provide accountability on a regular basis.

Today is the time to take up the challenge and start acting on what is tugging at your heart.

Some of you might still be thinking, *I don't want to step out of the boat and into something new.* I understand. Not everyone is going to respond to God at the same pace. Be wise and think about all that's involved, but let me encourage you to not let the unknown hold you back.

Pray, risk, and move forward in faith. God is with you, his plans are always for good, and you only have one life to live for him.

> *Trust in the Lord with all your heart and lean not on your own understanding; in all your ways acknowledge him, and he will make your paths straight.* (Proverbs 3:5-6)

May I Pray For You?

Heavenly Father, we are so easily drawn away, wanting what our culture says we need to be fulfilled. Help us to seek first your kingdom, your desires for our lives, and your plans for the one life we have from you.

Lord, teach us to trust you, to pray with anticipation, and to watch your guiding hand on our lives. Give us perseverance to run the race you have marked out for us. Give us courage and wisdom and excitement to become all you desire. Move us, Holy Spirit, to *Go For It!* Amen

About the Author

Poppy Smith

Speaker, Author, Spiritual Life Coach

www.poppysmith.com

With her warm personality and passion for communicating life-changing truths, Poppy Smith inspires people nationally and internationally to thrive spiritually, personally, and relationally. She is a former Bible Study Fellowship Teacher with a Masters in Spiritual Formation and Direction. Poppy is also an award-winning author who writes to help readers grow strong in life's happy and hard places.

Made in the USA
Charleston, SC
03 October 2016